The Portable Queer

HOMO HISTORY

The Portable Queer series

by Erin McHugh

....

OUT OF THE MOUTHS OF QUEERS

A GAY IN THE LIFE

HOMO HISTORY

The Portable Queer

· ·

Erin McHugh

· ·

HOMO HISTORY

· ·

A Compilation of Events that
Shook and Shaped the Gay World

a alyson books
NEW YORK

PUBLISHED BY
ALYSON BOOKS
245 WEST 17TH STREET
NEW YORK, NY 10011

DISTRIBUTION IN THE UNITED KINGDOM BY
TURNAROUND PUBLISHER SERVICES LTD.
UNIT 3, OLYMPIA TRADING ESTATE
COBURG ROAD, WOOD GREEN
LONDON N22 6TZ ENGLAND

FIRST EDITION: OCTOBER 2007

07 08 09 10 11 a 10 9 8 7 6 5 4 3 2 1

ISBN: 1-59350-031-9
ISBN-13: 978-1-59350-031-3

LIBRARY OF CONGRESS
CATALOGING-IN-PUBLICATION
DATA ARE ON FILE.

COVER DESIGN BY VICTOR MINGOVITS
INTERIOR DESIGN BY VICTOR MINGOVITS

Contents

Introduction

HOW DO YOU WRITE the history of a secret?

As long as there have been *homo sapiens*, there have been homosexuals. Yet how we have been viewed by the rest of society throughout the centuries has run the gamut: from pariahs and pederasts to—in a good century—emperors and kings. History has been an extremely precipitous roller coaster ride for gays, lesbians, bisexuals, and transgendered people, and though presently things in many parts of the world look somewhat brighter, experience tells us that social mores tend to change nearly as often as peoples' minds.

This volume hopes to show a little bit of the ride so far: the ancient Greeks and their student-lovers; gay monarchs through the ages; the horrors brought on by Germany's Paragraph 175; the legal trials of Irish playwright Oscar Wilde; the scandal of reparative therapy; the travesty of disallowing gays in the military. All historic steps in what we hope will become a more understanding, open-minded world.

Because there are signs of celebration as well. The advances just in the last century, post-Stonewall, such as gay pride, the Gay Games, National Coming Out Day. And sprinkled over time are mind-changing (and sometimes mind-blowing) moments: the bombshell that was The Kinsey Reports; the glory, mixed with heartache, of the AIDS Quilt; the publication of *The Well of Loneliness.*

But they are pinpricks, bits of time over eons of history—and history needs to be recorded, whether orally or by transcription, to offer insight into the past and a glimmer into the future. We have been a people who have had to hide ourselves and our history. But the secret is out now, and it remains up to us to keep it that way.

The Portable Queer

BACK IN THE DAY

HOMOSEXUALITY IN ANCIENT TIMES

THERE EXISTS TODAY a rather glamorous picture of both ancient Greece and Rome as gay playgrounds. A time of gigantic orgies amid Mediterranean delights. Lots of servants, gallons of wine. Well, some of that is true, but it wasn't exactly a night at the disco.

In general, it would be correct to call it same-sex love rather than what we presently think of as gay love. True, in Greece sex between men was not at all frowned upon, but it had its parameters. The relationships which were considered appropriate and even suitable were pederastic in nature, though they did not involve very young children; the younger partner was usually from thirteen to twenty years old, and the bond was very much a teacher-student affair—never exclusively sexual.

Nor did same-sex relations automatically signify that a man was a homosexual like they do today; it was not quite so simple. What identified a man was not the sex of the person he slept with as much as his lover's social standing. A Greek of high social standing would never be penetrated sexually: that was part of his status. And it didn't matter who he slept with—woman, slave, foreigner, young man—as long as it was the partner who was physically penetrated; to reverse positions would be shameful.

As far as men and boys were concerned, the relationship would be much akin to what we would think of as having a mentor today. A young man might be pursued by many older gentlemen, and would choose one for the duration. Education played as large a part in this bond as the erotic. The goal of any Greek education was a combination of both physical and mental perfection—this *is* the home of the Olympics, after all. The Greeks felt these arrangements kept crime down among the young by means of this caregiver relationship—and it also was a form of population control.

The gymnasium was at the center of Greek life. Not only was it used for physical exercise, but it was the intellectual heart of the town or city as well. Baths and places for what we would consider working out were part of the structure, of course, but they were also filled with artwork and statuary of Greek gods and war heroes. It was where the important people (read: men) of the town met: teachers, poets, and thinkers of all types. Here both the boys and men came together to hone their intellect and carve living sculptures of their bodies. Some of the greats of ancient Greece—and by great, we mean great homosexuals—gathered in such places: Plato, Herodotus, Xenophon, and many others. In literature, the first time we witnessed such a relationship was between Achilles and Patroclus in the *Iliad*, written in 800 BCE. Historians now believe these pederastic practices were common from that time until the Roman era. Modern study of this phenomenon began in the early twentieth century by Erich Bethe in 1907, and intensified by the 1970s with the publications of *Greek Homosexuality* by Kenneth Dover in 1978.

Most ironic of all, as we muddle through in an age of "Don't Ask, Don't Tell," homosexuality in the military of Ancient Greece was not only condoned, but considered beneficial. The most renowned example of this practice was the Sacred Band of Thebes, a fighting machine of 150 pederastic couples who served as the elite force of the Theban army. It was formed in 378 BCE by Gorgidas, the Theban commander, and existed for forty years, until their decimation in 338 BCE in the battle of Chaeronea. Believe it or not, the Greeks thought that using these couples—fighting together—boosted morale and improved fighting skills and brave behavior. A very modern approach to military strategy indeed.

The Romans were of a very different mind in the years of the Roman Republic. During much of that time, from 509 BCE–27 BCE, homosexual relations with a slave were still allowed, and bisexuality was tolerated, but a life entirely lived as a homosexual was considered immoral. By 226 CE, Lex Scantia, the first law forbidding sodomy, was put in place, and even consensual homosexual sex was banned.

Times change, of course, and homosexuality does not just disappear. Nero, who reigned from 37 CE–68 CE, seems to be the first Roman emperor to have married a male, and of the first dozen Roman emperors, only Claudius was completely heterosexual. A temple recently discovered outside of Rome most likely dates to 134 BCE, and is dedicated to emperor

Hadrian's lover Antinous; it seems to be a sort of homosexual retreat. Historians feel this was perhaps the last of the high times for gay Romans.

And as for lesbians: well, the Greeks had Sappho, but the Romans believed such girl action to be beyond the pale.

GAY MONARCHY

SO MANY HAVE STRAYED from the straight and narrow path over the centuries—and many of them were ruling their country (several of which had laws that punished homosexuals severely). Ah, for the good old days, when kings were queens and had plenty of time and power to do what they wanted without the media and paparazzi nipping at their heels.

Here are just a few tidbits of some of royalty's private lives:

RICHARD I OF ENGLAND (1157–1199)
This quote, from Roger of Hovedon, the King's biographer, pretty much says it all:

"Richard, [then] duke of Aquitaine, the son of the

king of England, remained with Philip, the King of France, who so honored him for so long that they ate every day at the same table and from the same dish, and at night their beds did not separate them. And the king of France loved him as his own soul; and they loved each other so much that the king of England was absolutely astonished at the passionate love between them and marveled at it."

EDWARD II OF ENGLAND (1284–1327)

This is a king who abhorred jousting, military strategy and other monarchal interests, preferring musicals and puttering in the garden. Cuckolded by his wife Isabella, who had other plans for who she'd prefer to live with in the castle (lover Roger de Mortimer), he was finally disposed of when he was captured and had a red-hot poker inserted in his anus. What a way to go.

MAGNUS ERIKSSON, MAGNUS IV OF SWEDEN (1316–1374)

Magnus was King of both Norway and Sweden, and married to Queen Blanche of Namur, when he was correctly accused of being a homosexual by his tattletale cousin, soon-to-be St. Bridget of Sweden. She found that he was sleeping with his favorite knight, Bengt Algotsson, and vilified him for "loving men more than God or your own soul or your spouse."

What could one expect from a King whose nickname was "Magnus Smek," which means "Pet-Magnus."

HENRI III OF FRANCE (1551–1589)

Though he did plenty right, it seems Henry just couldn't win.

He was extremely assiduous as a monarch, and very cultured and refined in a country that was bawdy and crude (though perhaps he *was* a bit too refined for some of his subjects). He was even a loving husband to his wife, Louise of Lorraine.

But in his constituents' eyes, all they saw was that Henry threw it all away. He had a brilliant military career that he tossed aside out of disinterest. Pamphlets circulated, accusing him of being a tyrant and having disturbing sexual tastes. Henry didn't help his own case much: he loved dressing in drag for a masked ball, hung around mostly with minions and writers, and wore way too much jewelry for the common man's tastes. And if that isn't convincing enough, he had a collection of tiny dogs, plus he hid in the castle cellars during thunderstorms.

JAMES I OF ENGLAND
(JAMES VI OF SCOTLAND) (1603–1625)

James was so open about his homosexuality that his subjects were apt to shout "Long live Queen James!" when raising a glass for a toast. In fact, it is reputed that the common joke at the time was, "Elizabeth was King: now James is Queen."

James took on both homosexuality and Jesus Christ in an address to the Privy Council in 1617. Imagine how this went over with the churchy crowd:

"I, James, am neither a god nor an angel, but a man like any other. Therefore I act like a man and confess to loving those dear to me more than other men. You may be sure that I love the Earl of Buckingham more than anyone else, and more than you who are here assembled. I wish to speak in my own behalf and not to have it thought to be a defect, for Jesus Christ did the same, and therefore I cannot be blamed. Christ had John, and I have George."

LUDWIG II OF BAVARIA (1845–1886)

Here was a king who is so busy being an opera queen he couldn't be bothered to see his troops off to war. Nor was he much for love with the ladies. He enjoyed a close relationship in his youth with Prince Paul von Thurn und Taxis. They seemed perfect for each other—long walks, reciting poetry, sharing their love of opera. But when Ludwig learned the Prince was taking out ladies on the side, he put an end to the love fest. The kingdom hoped for a new queen—in the royal and female sense of the word—to make an appearance; after years of obvious disinterest, Ludwig was betrothed to his cousin, Sophie. The nuptials were postponed twice, everyone finally got the message, and the engagement just quietly went away.

It turned out that Ludwig's other great love was—aside from opera—architecture, so he spent his monarchal time building some truly fabulous castles around Bavaria. But he had become more and more reclusive over the years—he occasionally gave wicked parties in his homes, with half-dressed stable boys and the soldiers, or went on romantic moonlit picnics with these always stunning young men. But aside from these forays, he remained alone, and rumors started to circulate about his mental stability.

He began to be known as "Ludwig the Mad," and his diaries show that his homosexuality disturbed him deeply. On a walk one evening with his psychiatrist, they both disappeared, only to be found in the lake the following day; the circumstances of their deaths remain a mystery even to this day. And though he was long absent from his regular magisterial duties, and thought more of Wagner's "Ring Cycle" than military marches, Ludwig remained popular in his subjects' minds, and they deeply mourned his passing.

AMERICA'S FIRST LESBIAN CONVICTION

IN SOME WAYS, things have improved considerably in the realm of lesbian rights. In the Untied States, it appears there hasn't been a conviction for being a lesbian since 1649. In fact, that seems to be the first, last, and only scarlet letter for the American girls.

Plymouth Colony was the site of many firsts and experiments in the New World for the Pilgrims in the seventeenth century, but one doesn't usually think of sexual hijinx as high on the list. Yet in 1649, two young women, Sarah White Norman and Mary Vincent Hammon, broke new ground in North America for being convicted for lesbian activity. Their "leude behauior each with other vpon a bed" set tongues a-wagging and landed them both in a mess. The charges against Hammond were dropped—though she was married, she was a mere fifteen years old—and Norman, upon her conviction, was forced to make a public confession. Norman, who was several years older than her paramour, would have another run-in of a sexual nature with the police. She had evidently been abandoned by her husband even before the gal pal incident, and later was accused (though was never convicted) of "sodomy & other vnclean practisses" with a local man.

The good news and the bad about the lack of legal action against lesbians in the U.S. is that lesbianism, as it has been throughout history, tends to be invisible. For men, according to United States law, sodomy was a capital crime, and execution was not out of the question. According to the books, sodomy required both penetration and "effusion of seed;" the same went for adultery and fornication arrests. Thus, if there were no male involved in the sexual act in question…well, there couldn't have been any sex! The women from Plymouth, therefore, could be punished for their conduct, but not for a sex crime. This sort of thinking goes back as far as the Talmud, and was common around the world well into the twentieth century.

William Bradford, the Massachusetts governor at the time of the Hammon-Norman incident, believed the devil himself was attempting to corrupt the people of Plymouth—they who had just come to start a new life. He thought it was because his constituents were so especially virtuous. Bradford wrote that the prevalence of wickedness should "cause us to fear and tremble at the consideration of our corrupte natures." What would he have thought, to see that in over 350 years, lesbians are still running free—as are their friendly male sodomite friends?

BOSTON MARRIAGE

RARELY HAVE TWO WORDS had such a checkered, fascinating history. The original use of the phrase "Boston marriage" was most likely literary, referring to the relationship between two women in Henry James' novel, *The Bostonians*, published in 1886. In his book, a pair of women lived together and enjoyed a very close, intimate relationship; they were called "New Women" at the time, indicating their emotional and financial independence from men. Historians have long thought that James' fictional couple was modeled on the real-life relationship of writer Sarah Orne Jewett and Annie Adams Fields. From the time of the publication of James' book to the present, however, it has consistently been suggested that both the fictional couple and Jewett and Fields were also engaged in a discreet lesbian relationship. Opinions have differed.

Fast forward to 1999. David Mamet writes a play called—what else?—*Boston Marriage*, and the two Victorian leads are very lesbian indeed. The meaning of the phrase starts to evolve, and people begin to assume that "Boston marriage" (the living arrangement, not the play) has *always* been a wink-and-a-nod way of saying "lesbians living together undercover."

But there's one more twist: in 2004, Massachusetts became the first state in the U.S. to allow same-sex marriages. Boston being the only major city that allowed same-sex marriage, the expression took on yet another new life: now people assumed it meant legal same-sex marriages. It is also currently in use by some to mean a lesbian relationship that was formerly sexual, and now merely a comfortable marriage of convenience. What next?

PARAGRAPH 175

IN GERMANY, THE LAST PART of the nineteenth century and nearly the entirety of the twentieth were scarred by the existence of an abominable law known as Paragraph 175—or formally as §175 StGB. Part of the German Criminal Code, it deemed any acts between males, consenting or not, a crime; the specifics of the law were so outmoded that early versions also featured bestiality.

The original article against Unnatural Fornication, passed on May 15, 1871, read:

Unnatural fornication, whether between persons of the male sex or of humans with beasts, is to be punished by imprisonment; a sentence of loss of civil rights may also be passed.

Almost since it was enacted, there were movements to have Paragraph 175 stricken from the books; as early as the 1890s, it was referred to as the "disgraceful paragraph." Again between 1919 and 1933, during the time of the Weimar Republic, liberals fought against it, joining a growing worldwide effort to change or repeal anti-homosexual laws. But despite extremely open attitudes towards gay lifestyle in parts of Germany—especially Berlin—they could not manage a parliamentary majority. And the worst was still to come.

The Nazis were soon in power. Hitler's fear of homosexuals took a grim hold in the Third Reich, and Paragraph 175 became a very useful law for their persecution. It was broadened further to include "lewd acts," which left interpretation wide open; sexual conduct that did not even include physical contact, like masturbation in another's company, was prosecuted. Before long, men were convicted simply on suspected behavior, and historians believe that as many as 100,000 were sent to prisons or concentration camps. Many of these men were captured by the Gestapo via "pink lists," their names simply gathered by neighbors or acquaintances who reported people they suspected as homosexual. It is believed that fewer than 4,000 of these prisoners survived. Those who perished constitute one of the highest mortality rates of any non-Jewish prisoner factions in the camps.

Oddly, Paragraph 175 did not mention—and therefore did not ban—sexual acts between women. Though it was firmly believed that gay men would poison the growth of Hitler's perfect Aryan culture, the fact that lesbians wouldn't be procreating with heterosexual Aryan men did not seem to be part of the Nazi equation. Lesbian bars and clubs were shut down, but that seems to be the extent of their persecution during this era.

But the end of Word War II still did not bring

the end of Paragraph 175. Between 1945 and 1969, about 50,000 more men were convicted and sentenced because of this horrific legislation. East and West Germany followed different versions of the law after World War II ended. East Germany originally utilized the old version for several years, limited the punishment to include only sex with young men under eighteen in 1968, and dispensed with the law altogether in 1988. West Germany followed the Nazi version until 1969, and finally dissolved Paragraph 175 in 1994 upon the reunification of Germany.

Gay activists began in earnest as early as 1973 to have Paragraph 175 revoked, and during their quest, began to document the stories of gay men who were imprisoned during the War because of it. They found that "The 175ers," as they were labeled, were often treated in the camps as medical cases, and therefore became the subjects of scientific experimentation. "Cures" to make a prisoner heterosexual (such as an operation to insert a capsule that released testosterone) caused illness and even death—and, it comes as no surprise, no new scientific answers. Castration was considered a cure, too. Some prisoners agreed to this option in return for a promise of leniency; later, however, homosexuals were often castrated at the whim of the camp officials.

On May 15, 2002 (a date chosen for its numerical significance—17.5), the German Bundestag vacated convictions of Paragraph 175 at last by passing a supplemental law. Gay activist groups remained dissatisfied, however, as this cleared convictions from the Nazi years only, and not post-World War II arrests.

An extremely moving film called *Paragraph 175*, by Rob Epstein and Jeffrey Friedman, was released to great acclaim in 2002. In this haunting documentary, five survivors of Nazi concentration camps, arrested for the crime of being homosexual, unfold their heartbreaking stories of horror and survival, a testament of both human fortitude and "the love that dare not speak its name."

THE NIGHT OF THE LONG KNIVES

WHETHER YOU CALL IT *Nacht de langen Messer*, "Operation Hummingbird," The Night of the Long

Knives—some even call it a Gay Kristellnacht—it was one of Hitler's earliest annihilations of a group that was interfering with his grasp for power.

The Sturmabteilung, known as the SA, was originally Hitler's strong-arm group during his rise in the 1920s. Also known as Stormtroopers or Brownshirts, they proved invaluable right up until his appointment as German chancellor in 1933. But shortly after this, disenchantment grew on the parts of both the SA and the new leader who had formerly championed them.

The SA began to feel that Hitler had forgotten the socialist principles that he had promised the new Nazi leadership would support; he had started to form a more nationalistic view. They felt betrayed, and Hitler began to hear talk of a "second revolution" by the SA. He had given them power, and now he feared they would destroy him in a coup. The SA had grown to a force of about 700,00 men by then, most of them from the working class.

Hitler realized that political infighting would help his cause. His advisors—Hermann Goring, Joseph Goebbels, Heinrich Himmler and others—were unhappy with the reign, and especially the influence of SA leader Ernst Röhm. They felt—and Hitler was beginning to agree—that the troops that had been so dedicated to Der Führer had become no more than thugs. They were drunks, extortionists, and very bawdy, and the German people were beginning to both hate and fear them—in short, not a showcase for what Hitler wanted for his new regime. Unfortunately, Röhm, who was openly homosexual, was a longtime friend of Hitler's and one of his earliest henchmen, so this caused a problem.

The new chancellor realized that he needed a different ilk of support behind him; he also needed higher profile friends: generals, industry leaders and other bigwigs who understood his long-range plan of more than just a socialist republic, but a world superpower. The SS—or Schutzstaffel—which was a faction of the SA, became Hitler's new darlings, and Hitler called Röhm in for a meeting to set things straight. The SA would no longer be the ultimate military force in the new Germany, he informed him, but be limited to political functions only. Röhm reluctantly accepted Hitler's decision. Naturally, this later helped fuel the false rumors that Himmler and

Heydrich would whisper into Der Führer's ear—
that Röhm was planning a coup against his former
mentor.

So with a heavy heart Hitler accompanied the SS
on June 29, 1934, to a hotel at Wiesse, where Röhm
and many of his officers—who were also highly criti-
cized by Hitler's henchmen for being known homosexuals—were gathered for a retreat. Thus began a
bloodbath of the old SA leadership that continued
for two weeks. Hitler, for once sentimental, balked
at killing Ernst Röhm, wanting to pardon him, but
Goring and Himmler convinced him otherwise.
So out of respect, Hitler gave Röhm a gun with a
single bullet, and left his old friend alone in a room
to commit suicide. Hitler is said to have wept upon
signing Röhm's death warrant. Röhm allegedly said
to his executioners, "If I am to be killed, let Adolf do
it himself." When, after fifteen minutes, Röhm was
found to still be alive, he was shot twice by the SS.
His last words were reputed to be, "Mein Führer,
mein Führer!"

Official records show that eighty-two men died
that weekend at the hands of the new regime, and

that Hitler, who had been the subject of gay rumors himself, told the public that many of the men were homosexual, and a danger to Germany. It's likely that the deaths were actually upwards of 200, eliminating most of the SA leadership, a number of homosexuals, and various others who might pose a problem to the new Nazi regime. It was named "The Night of Long Knives" after a massacre in Arthurian legend, though this was indeed no fairy tale.

The SS remained by Hitler's side as the SA's members diminished, gradually disappearing altogether. Of this shameful bloodbath, Hitler said:

"If anyone reproaches me and asks why I did not resort to the regular courts of justice, then all I can say is this: In this hour I was responsible for the fate of the German people, and thereby I became the supreme judge of the German people."

He had now put himself above the law, on a pedestal of maniacal narcissism and psychosis that he would stand upon until his death. And it also began Hitler's slaughter of homosexuals, which would continue through more than a decade in concentration camps and beyond.

An addendum: on a weekend exactly thirty-five years later, the Stonewall Riots would take place in New York City.

ALCATRAZ'S FIRST PRISONER

"THE ROCK" GAINED ITS real notoriety long after it first opened its gates. The island in the middle of shimmering San Francisco Bay was discovered in 1775 by Juan de Ayala, who named it "La Isla de los Alcatraces," meaning "Island of the Pelicans." But it has had a checkered history: a lighthouse, a Civil War prison, the place where most prisoners were brought after the 1906 San Francisco earthquake decimated the city, and in 1911, the United States Disciplinary Barracks.

From the 1930s into the 1960s, however, Alcatraz, as it was now simply called, became perhaps the toughest maximum-security prison in the United States, home to the nation's most dangerous and incorrigible men, people like Al Capone, George "Machine Gun" Kelly, Alvin Karpis, members of Ma

Barker's gang, and many, many more.

What the general public does not know is that some of these "dangerous and incorrigible" criminals went there for another punishable crime: sodomy. One of our country's more shameful moments— gazing out over the gentle hills of San Francisco, of all places!—was the incarceration of the very first Alcatraz prisoner on July 1, 1934. Frank Bolt, Federal Prisoner #1, was an Army officer convicted and imprisoned for being caught in a homosexual act: he received a five-year sentence for sodomy. In fact, nine out of the first twenty-five prisoners brought to The Rock were jailed for sodomy. Now *that's* criminal.

THE HOMOPHILE MOVEMENT

BEFORE THE RISE OF what we call the gay rights movement came the homophile movement, its vaguely sinister-sounding predecessor. But the word *homophile* is a now little-used synonym for homosexual, and was chosen to identify the movement because the "-phile" suffix from the Greek emphasizes love, rather than sex. In the 1950s and 1960s, the nascent movement began to organize, forming both men's and women's groups (in those days things in the gay community were most often divided by sex) to gain strength and strategize about civil rights.

These early organizations used picketing, protests, their own magazines and newspapers and the like to spread the word; the leaders of these groups were mostly well-educated white professionals, savvy about political and social change. The first recorded demonstration for gay rights took place in 1962, when Craig Rodwell (who later opened the famous Oscar Wilde Bookstore) and Randy Wicker picketed in front of New York City's draft board offices. This was three decades before "Don't Ask, Don't Tell," of course, so it was not about gays in the military; these men were protesting the policy of releasing draft-age men's information on their sexual orientation to employers.

However, European activists had quite a jump on the Americans. Activist Adolf Brand led a German homosexual liberation movement and published the first gay literary and artistic journal in history. *Der*

Eigene (The Self-Owner) first went to press in 1896, and was available until 1931, with a subscriber base thought to reach about 1,500 per issue. The onset of World War II, coupled with Adolph Hitler's open persecution of gay men, led to several quiet years for the burgeoning homophile movement in Europe. But by 1943, Swiss actor Karl Meier, who went under the pseudonym "Rolf," was publishing *Der Kreis*, which became the leading European publication for homophiles from 1943 to 1967. Action in Denmark, the Netherlands, Sweden, England, and throughout Europe began to bubble.

By the 1950s, the two major organizations for gay men and women—the Mattachine Society and The Daughters of Bilitis, respectively—were growing strong in the United States. They were still somewhat conservative and secret, however, and when the 1960s came in with a bang, the homophile movement began to take lessons from then-powerful groups like the black civil rights movement and women's liberation. The Homophile Youth Movement in Neighborhoods (HYMN) had taken hold in New York City by late 1967—and these kids were already shouting "Gay

Power!" and "Gay is Good!" for everyone to hear. The gloves were off. Suddenly people were talking about "gay liberation," and from the late 1960s through the 1970s, men and women in North America, Western Europe, Australia and New Zealand began to come out of the closet and get into the streets. The days of secret meetings and plain brown wrappers were over. We were here, we were queer, and people were going to have to get used to it.

EARLY AMERICAN HOMOPHILE ORGANIZATIONS

MATTACHINE SOCIETY

It was November 11, 1950, and the second half of the century was about to bring a huge change to the bubbling undercurrent demanding equality and gay rights in the United States. A small group of men—soon-to-be-activists—gathered to begin a call for change: led by Harry Hay, they also included Chuck Rowland, Dale Jennings, Bob Hull, and Rudi Gernreich. They called themselves the Mattachine Society, a name Hay had run across while doing some research; the Mattachines had been a French medieval and Renaissance masque group. Hay explained just why he thought the name was the perfect fit for the nascent group in a 1976 interview:

"We took the name Mattachine because we felt that we 1950s Gays were also a masked people, unknown and anonymous, who might become engaged in morale building and helping ourselves and others, through struggle, to move toward total redress and change."

The original Mattacino was a fictional court jester in Italian theater who always told his king the truth when no one else would speak up. The new name would fit America's first homophile organization perfectly.

The Mattachine Society began to gain some footing in the early 1950s, but the original core members were all Marxists, and this tie to Communism during the time of the Red Scare would soon hurt both their growth and their profile profoundly. New people were reticent to become members—being labeled both a homosexual and a Communist automatically made a person a security risk in the eyes of the U.S. government—so the group distanced themselves from any Communist leanings. For this reason, Harry Hay, a dedicated Communist, resigned as the Mattachine's leader in 1954, and the group began to look towards the black civil rights movement and other human rights organizations for models of success.

Even with its new leadership in place, however, the Mattachine Society was seen as fairly conservative in their actions. They spoke of liberating the oppressed, published a magazine for members called *The Mattachine Review*, began to set up legal and other referral services, and lobbied against discrimination and the repeal of sodomy laws. Still, they had a rather old-fashioned mission statement that read in part that homosexuals' "physiological and psychological handicaps need be no deterrent in integrating ten percent of the world's population towards the constructive social progress of mankind." Many gay people began to understand that more radical action needed to be taken, and interest in what had been a groundbreaking political group began to wane. Sadly, infighting among the leadership about the direction of the organization brought its demise in 1961, just over a decade after it had been founded.

ONE, INCORPORATED

Some of the Mattachine Society's internal problems led, fortunately, to better things for the burgeoning gay rights movement. In 1952, Mattachine's Chuck Rowland and Dale Jennings joined with Donald Slater, W. Dorr Legg, Martien Block, and Tony Reyes and founded ONE, Incorporated, whose name came from a quote from Thomas Carlyle: "A mystic bond of brotherhood that makes all men one."

Things were different at ONE. They were the first homophile organization to actually open a public office, right there for all the world to see, on the streets of Los Angeles. It quickly became a makeshift community center. Out of these offices also came *ONE* magazine in 1953, full of essays, book reviews and other features interesting to the gay reader, including news from around the world about other people, organizations and political action and strides just like the homophile movement in the U.S. was experiencing. It was an instant must-have magazine, selling out of gay bars and on the streets of LA for twenty-five cents, and eventually enjoyed a nationwide circulation of 5,000 by the end of the 1950s.

But on the road to its success as a magazine, the postmaster of Los Angeles intervened. The post office stopped shipment of the October 1954 issue, labeling it "obscene, lewd, lascivious, and filthy." The homophile movement was getting mad and they were getting serious: ONE, Inc. sued, and the case went all the way to the United States Supreme Court. It took four years, but the Supreme Court overturned two earlier rulings, and ruled that gay publications were not, per se, obscene. It was one of the first huge wins for what was beginning to be called the gay rights movement.

Unlike the Mattachine Society, ONE welcomed female members, and some of the women activists were crucial to its success, even in the very early years. The members also helped the Daughters of Bilitis when it was starting up, giving hard-earned advice, both political and, for the launch of *The Ladder*, editorial.

ONE, Inc. even had a paid employee in Legg, most likely the first ever in the new movement. And ONE was not just discussing and planning what could happen with gay rights among themselves—the community was right there in the room with them. They offered courses, lectures and guidance on life as a homosexual, and began a research library for homosexual studies; in 1956 the library became the basis for the ONE Institute of Homophile Studies, the first such academic institution of its kind in the United States. The new resource center continued to grow with the ONE Institute Quarterly of Homophile Studies, and after Legg's death in 1994, the ONE Institute, which was still in existence, merged with the International Gay and Lesbian Archives. In 2001, the ONE National Gay and Lesbian Archives opened a building of their own, donated by the University of Southern California. More than fifty years after ONE, Inc. was founded, it has a home where its original mission statement is realized every day, dedicating itself to "collecting, preserving, documenting, studying, and communicating our history, our challenges, and our aspirations."

DAUGHTERS OF BILITIS

In 1955, a little organization popped up in San Francisco, with a few women talking about lesbian rights and publishing a small newspaper. The group was called The Daughters of Bilitis, and the publication, which would offer lesbians an entirely new reading experience about others like themselves, was *The Ladder*. Suddenly, there was a world for a certain type of woman that strode bravely between the illegal lesbian bar scene and ladies' meat loaf recipe-trading magazines.

It was still the 1950s, of course, so it wasn't as if women were coming out in force yet. But there were pockets of like-minded women all over the nation, and chapters of the DOB started to sprout up. Bars were always a little dangerous to go to—arrest was never out of the question—and not to everyone's taste. And once *The Ladder* began to roll off the presses in 1956, full of news, letters from readers, short stories and poetry, as well as updates on new chapters of the DOB, their meetings and social activities, lesbians truly had a place to gather—if not in person, then at least through the pages of this incredible publication.

The Daughters of Bilitis was founded by activists Del Martin and her partner, Phyllis Lyon; Lyon also took on editorial duties at *The Ladder*. It is considered the first lesbian rights organization to be formed in the United States; evidently they had no idea that male homophile groups like the Mattachine Society were also beginning to gather around the country as well. Clearly, the times they were a-changing—and they couldn't, and wouldn't, be stopped.

The name of the organization stemmed from a book written in 1894 by French poet Pierre Louis. *The Songs of Bilitis* featured a fictional character named Bilitis, who was a contemporary of Sappho, the Greek poetess. *The Ladder* was meant to be an answer to Radclyffe Hall's 1928 lesbian novel, *The Well of Loneliness.* Lyon and other members of DOB hoped that *The Ladder*, which started as a modest 12-page newsletter, would be a way up and out of the "well" that Hall spoke so movingly about. It became a benchmark and a truly liberating force for gay women. They were able to communicate with each other through letters and commentary, and high-profile writers (though at first some of them used pseudonyms) began to contribute, like novelist May Sarton, science fiction author Marion Zimmer Bradley, playwright Lorraine Hansberry, and Ann Weldy, who was already using a pseudonym of her own, in the person of pulp novelist Ann Bannon.

In 1963, the editorship of *The Ladder* was handed over to Philadelphia activist Barbara Gittings. Circulation had grown to over 4,000, and it was actually sold on newsstands in major cities. It is likely that the readership was much, much higher than the reported subscription base. These were the plain-brown-wrapper days, and the pass-along factor was certainly huge; the number of women who actually read each issue was surely many times the circulation number back at *The Ladder* offices. Even more astonishing were the covers that came to be *The Ladder's* signature after Gittings took the helm. The new editor's partner, Kay Tobin Lahusen, shot photographs of ordinary women that began to grace the cover of each issue. Essentially these women were outing themselves to the world: this, in 1950s America! The bravery of lesbian activists was beginning to show, and in the most unusual ways.

But feminism was beginning to play its part in women's rights, too, and instead of helping the lesbian rights cause, it became a disturbingly divisive factor. It was very difficult to get women involved in the lesbian rights movement in those early days anyway. Going to meetings and reading a newsletter in order to understand yourself and encounter other like people was one thing; attending marches and protests was another. But the feminists were coming out of their own closet in droves—and they were decidedly anti-lesbian. The new feminist movement was making great strides in society, the workplace, even the home, but their strident "Move over, guys" attitude drew the usual anti-lesbian remarks form the public, especially men. The feminists were eager to detach themselves from the lesbian rights faction. It's also highly probable that women who identified as lesbians, but were not ready to jump out of the closet as activists, joined forces with the feminists in order to make some headway in the equal rights arena. All this added up to rifts within the DOB ranks, and a precipitous drop in membership nationwide. At their own national convention in 1970, the Daughters of Bilitis closed their doors. *The Ladder* ceased publication soon after, in 1972.

But there was good news on the horizon: the unthinkable was about to happen. Men and women started to join forces and fight for gay rights together, as a cohesive unit. The real fight was about to begin…

The Portable Queer

MILESTONES

ULRICHS' URNINGS

KARL HEINRICHS ULRICHS (1825-1895), a brilliant German jurist, began to write about his thoughts on homosexuality in the 1860s. In doing so, he lost his job, most likely became the first person in history to out himself—and, in his case, suffer the consequences—and gave rise to the scientific study of homosexuality that continues today.

Ulrichs wrote a dozen pamphlets on homosexuality, or what he called "The Riddle of Man-Manly Love." He first began publishing under the pseudonym of Numa Numantius in order to protect his family, but in time he reverted to using his real name. Ulrichs is often cited as the first real gay activist.

Ulrichs developed a sort of "language of love" about homosexuals; that is, he devised a set of words to at last define the different faces of sexual desire for this group of people that no one previously had spoken out about. He was the first to describe his own feelings—and therefore the feelings of countless others—that he saw himself as a kind of "hermaphrodite of the mind"—a female psyche in a male body. At

that time, the scientific community was just beginning to call homosexuals (though the word not yet
in use) a kind of "third sex." Since this was a behavior determined by the mind, Ulrichs insisted that
laws that might provoke criminal proceedings, like
Germany's Paragraph 175, which forbade the sexual
practices of Urnings, as he called these people, were
unjust. (The word "homosexual" was not used until
1869 in a pamphlet which was published by human
rights activist Karl-Maria Kertbeny, though he wrote
anonymously at the time.)

Ulrichs chose the name Urning from the Greek
classics. In Plato's Symposium, there is a discussion
of the birth of Aphrodite, the goddess of love. One
version has her born of Uranus—the heavens. In this
mythological version, the female plays no part in the
birth; this Unranian Aphrodite speaks of a noble love
for male youth.

So Ulrichs' Uranians originally referred to men
"with a female psyche" who were sexually attracted
to other men; later, Ulrichs would realize that all
male sexual relationships did not necessarily have a
female component, and he developed a more com-

plex language that relied on sexual orientation, pre-
ferred sexual behavior, and gender characteristics.

Although Ulrichs' language of Uranians was soon
outdated and nearly extinct, it was the first time it
had been described and discussed at all. Some of
Ulrichs most utilized sexual terms are:

URNING: *A male-bodied person with a*
female psyche, whose main sexual attraction
is to men

URNINGIN: *A female-bodied person with a*
male psyche, whose main sexual attraction
is to women

DIONINGIN: *A heterosexual woman*

DIONING: *A heterosexual man*

URANODIONING: *A male bisexual*

URANODIONINGIN: *A female bisexual*

ZWITTER: *An intersexual, or what we might*
call a hermaphrodite

ZWISCHEN-URNING: *An adult male who*
prefers adolescent males; a pederast

URANIASTER: *A heterosexual engaging in*
situational homosexuality

Ulrichs' language—especially the term Urning—did gain some notoriety for a while among a small poetry movement in England's late Victorian age through the 1930s. Uranian poetry spoke primarily of pederasty, though in quite a covert manner, so as not to alert British authorities.

Though Ulrich's studies, theories, and especially his language, seem hopelessly outdated in many ways, his ideas were cutting edge. He promoted coming out, and had his own very difficult experience to speak to—including its very positive results; he insisted Urnings deserved equal rights; spoke to women's rights in the same manner; and perhaps most importantly, insisted that gay people were not diseased or criminal. As a jurist, he even outlined the by-laws for a gay rights organization. In short, our first real gay hero.

THE TRIALS OF OSCAR WILDE

THIS IS THE STORY OF how Ireland's most famous playwright brought a libel case against his nemesis—

only to have the tables turned so violently that he found himself in jail.

Born in Dublin in 1854, the pride of Trinity College, and one of the most celebrated wits of his (or any) time, Oscar Wilde suffered through perhaps the most painful unveiling of a person's sexual preference in modern times. Conjecture varies on when Wilde's extremely active homosexual—some even say pederastic—life began. In the main, historians agree that Wilde most likely had the same experiences common in many English public schools: group sexual encounters with other teenaged boys. He went on to marry and have two sons, but most believe that his serious homosexual life began after he had wed Constance Lloyd.

Wilde's life was filled with a combination of great theatrical success and lots of young men, many of them servants and rent boys. His longtime love, however, was Lord Alfred Douglas—"Bosie"—a situation that did not sit well with Lord Alfred's father, the powerful Marquess of Queensbury (yes, he of the Queensbury rules). Wilde's effete ways especially embarrassed Lord Alfred's father, so when Queensbury slandered Wilde publicly by leaving a calling card in a club for him with the message, "For Oscar Wilde, posing Somdomite " (*sic*), the dramatist sued him for libel and brought him to court.

It was, of course, a circus. Wilde's adversaries brought in young men from the streets to testify against him, hotel employees who bore witness to fecal stains on the bed sheets, and even wore down the great Wilde himself, a man never without a sharp riposte. But eventually Oscar Wilde not only lost his own libel case, but the judge had him arrested for "gross indecency." Wilde lost the suit and was sentenced to two years of hard labor. The judge declared, "People who can do these things must be dead to all sense of shame... It is the worst case I have ever tried."

"The love that dare not speak its name," as Lord Alfred Douglas called his relationship with Oscar Wilde, nearly killed the playwright. Wilde went to jail bankrupt, had lost both his theatrical and poetic audience, and was in ruinous health. By 1900, just two years out of prison, at the age of forty-six, the great Oscar Wilde was dead.

THE FIRST SEX-CHANGE OPERATION

LILI ELBE'S STORY BEGAN in 1882 as Elnar Wegener, born a Danish boy who grew up to be a successful and well-known artist who met a top-notch illustrator at the Copenhagen Art School, a woman named Gerda Gottlieb. In 1904, when Elnar was twenty-two and Gerda nineteen, they married.

Gerda was an Art Deco illustrator with a boom-ing business; one day, with a deadline looming and a model who failed to show up for a session, she goaded Elnar into taking the model's place. Wegener had extremely feminine features, and was often mis-taken for a girl in trousers on the street, so Gerda fig-ured she could make it work. Neither of them could have predicted what would happen.

Donning stockings and heels for Gerda, Elnar was instantly shocked at how right he felt in the new clothes, and how easy dressing and posing as a woman was for him. Legend has it that the model eventually showed up, and they quickly dubbed the "new girl" who stood there in her place as "Lili."

Elnar later added the surname Elbe, after the river he so loved.

Lili continued as Gerda's model for years, and is the subject of many of her most famous fashion illustrations. Close friends knew Lili was a transsexual, but for years she went out as Lili and entertained with Gerda as Lili, who introduced her to people as her sister.

In 1930, Elnar/Lili went to Germany for the first of five operations, most likely becoming the first person to have sex reassignment surgery. Her first surgery was for removal of the male genitals. Her doctor was the famed sexologist Magnus Hirschfield in Berlin. The other operations were done by Dr. Warnekros in Dresden, which included an ovaries transplant and later, a uterus transplant. Lili had hoped to have children and doctors indeed thought it possible. She and Gerda had by now gotten an annulment from the King of Denmark himself, she had a passport that read Lili Elbe, and had accepted a marriage proposal. What happened next will always remain a mystery: either Lili died in 1931 from complications connected to her last surgery, or she faked her own death and went off to live her new life in peace.

It is likely that Lili was intersex, and had Klinefelter's Syndrome, which is a male with an extra X chromosome (XXY). Both Lili and her doctors would have been in the dark about this at the time, as this condition was not medically recognized until 1942; it affects one in every 500-1,000 males.

Lili Elbe's story has lived on. In 1933 a book appeared named *Man into Woman*, written by Ernst Ludwig Hathom Jacobson under the pseudonym Niels Hoyer. Though the names in the book are changed, it is based on Lili's letters and diary entries, edited with her help before her disappearance or death. *Man into Woman* remains an important piece of literature in gender studies, as it is one of the first works to draw a distinction between homosexuality and transsexuality (or as current verbiage would have it, sexual orientation and gender identity). Elbe is also the subject of the award-winning 2000 novel *The Danish Girl*, by David Ebershoff.

THE WELL OF LONELINESS

BY THE 1950S, the jacket copy on this by then-famous novel called it "the strange love story of a girl who stood midway between the sexes." Today, its publicity copy calls it "the timeless story of a lesbian couple's struggle to be accepted by 'polite' society. Shockingly candid for its time, this novel was the very first to condemn homophobic society for its unfair treatment of gays and lesbians."

And what a long, strange trip it's been since Radclyffe Hall's *The Well of Loneliness* was first published in 1928...

By the time Hall wrote *The Well*, as it has been called by fans these many decades, she had had much success already as an author—enough that she thought she could take a chance with such steamy fare. She may have felt ready to expose this thinly veiled look at her own life as a lesbian, but the rest of the world, apparently, was not.

For the uninitiated, the novel introduces us to Stephen Mary Olivia Gertrude Gordon, an upper-class Englishwoman who lives life as an "invert"—a term used by sexologists-of-the-day like Havelock Ellis to describe a homosexual. Stephen, a World War I ambulance driver, falls in love with Mary Llewellyn. Mary returns her love, but their life is full of rejection and isolation, due to society's very negative view of their lifestyle. The novel actually makes a plea to the world at large: "Give us also the right to our existence." But it seemed no one was listening.

Dirty? Filthy? Pornographic and explicit? Not at all—there was not even a single sex scene in the novel. *The Well* began its long journey into scandal and banned bookdom because of this one phrase:

"And that night, they were not divided."

That was enough, however, for the British courts, who deemed it obscene as it promoted "unnatural practices between women." And though lesbianism was not a crime in England (mostly because Queen Victoria refused to believe in its very existence), they felt there was certainly no reason to put it on the bookshelves and give women pornographic ideas. If it remained in the stores, they reasoned, it would seem as if the government was condoning the idea that lesbians should have a real and meaningful place in the world.

The reviews of *The Well* were immediate and vit-
riolic, especially from James Douglas of the *Sunday
Express* in London, who wrote that he "would rather
give a healthy boy or a healthy girl a phial of prussic
acid than this novel." The words "unutterable putre-
faction" and "contagion" were also tossed in for good
measure.

In any case, *The Well* did not see a lot of shelf time
in the stores during its publication year of 1928. There
were seizures of product and a trial was launched, so
the editors at Jonathan Cape, Hall's British publisher,
sent papier-mâché molds of the type to a publisher in
Paris hoping they could figure a way to garner some
back-door sales. Books were printed in France, and
then sent back to England, where they were stopped
at customs. There wasn't much hope for *The Well* in
England: despite the support of literati such as Leon-
ard and Virginia Woolf, E.M. Forster, H.G. Wells,
George Bernard Shaw, Ethyl Smith, and T.S. Eliot,
the Home Secretary at the time, William Joyner-
Hicks, was reputed to be quite a conservative fellow.
Before he brought criminal proceedings against *The*

Well, he was busy cracking down on nightclubs, alcohol, gambling, and opposing a revised edition of *The Book of Common Prayer*. *The Well* would not be sold in the U.K.—not in the 1920s, at least. Even on appeal, it was labeled "obscene."

In New York, it may come as no surprise, things went a little differently. The book was reprinted six times before the case even came to trial. It was priced at five dollars—twice the price of a novel in those days—and sold 100,000 copies its first year in print. Though the American courts did go so far as to call it a "delicate social problem," they did not find it obscene. The United States Customs Court ruled that it didn't contain "one word, phrase, sentence or paragraph which could be truthfully pointed out as offensive to modesty."

Ever since *The Well*'s publication, readers have been divided about the portrayal of lesbians in the book. Though it is generally agreed that Radclyffe Hall took on the world in writing this first novel written by a lesbian that speaks openly about homosexuality, it is not considered high literature. Some say its butch and femme main characters did not help the public's view of lesbian stereotypes.

Yet *The Well of Loneliness* has been continuously in print since its original publication, been translated into fourteen languages, still sells tens of thousands every year, and for countless young women, has been the only book about lesbian love they had ever heard of while growing up—and quite possibly their initiation.

THE KINSEY REPORTS

THESE ARE THE SOURCE of the "10% of the population" figure that we all so freely use as a viable statistic for homosexuality. What's commonly referred to as The Kinsey Reports are actually two books: *Sexual Behavior in the Human Male*, published in 1948, and *Sexual Behavior in the Human Female*, from 1953. They were written by Alfred Kinsey, a biologist and zoologist who founded the Institute for Research in Sex, Gender and Reproduction at Indiana University, where he was a professor.

Kinsey's findings rocked not only the scientific world, but also the general public's idea of sexual practices in America. And one of the greatest taboos Kinsey tackled in his books was the prevalence of homosexuality. He believed not only that people had sexual fantasies and desires about people of their own sex, but acted on it with much more frequency than the public previously thought—for example, his sampling concluded that 37 percent of males and 13 percent of females had one or more orgasmic homosexual experience. Perhaps what was most shocking was the Kinsey Scale, which rated one's sexuality from 1-6:

0 : *Exclusively heterosexual with no homosexual*

1 : *Predominantly heterosexual,*
only incidentally homosexual

2 : *Predominantly heterosexual,*
but more than incidentally homosexual

3 : *Equally heterosexual and homosexual*

4 : *Predominantly homosexual,*
but more than incidentally heterosexual

5 : *Predominantly homosexual,*
only incidentally heterosexual

6 : *Exclusively homosexual*

The books, the professor, the Scale—it blew the roof off people's idea of what was really going on in everyone else's bedroom. Controversy ensued: the sampling was too small, too tainted (there were a lot of male prisoners surveyed), too skewed. But the gloves were off—sex was suddenly out in the open. Remember, this was more than *two decades* before the American Psychological Association removed homosexuality from its list of mental disorders. Many social historians equate this sudden openness, courtesy of Kinsey, with the dawn of the sexual revolution of the 1960s.

The father of sexology died in 1956 with much work still to do; however, his successors at the Institute published *Homosexualities* in 1978, noting, "It goes beyond all the old stuff about inserter and insertee, butch and femme." Seems like old-fashioned stuff now, but to the general populace, it took very private, guilty fantasies and made them more permissible at last.

THE WORLD'S FIRST GAY BOOKSTORE

BEFORE THE STONEWALL RIOTS, before the Gay Liberation Front, and more than a decade before the scourge of AIDS, one of New York City's brightest lights opened its doors. The Oscar Wilde Bookstore now bills itself as "The World's Oldest Gay and Lesbian Bookstore," and it also often acted as a makeshift community center for the city's burgeoning gay movement.

Talk about something to be grateful for: it was Thanksgiving weekend of 1967, and gay activist Craig Rodwell opened a little literary storefront on Mercer Street named after a famed homosexual Irish playwright. Previously, the term "gay bookstore" meant dark windows, lots of pornography, and a back room. But the store Rodwell opened spoke volumes: Oscar Wilde carried real gay and lesbian literature and nonfiction, and actually refused to carry any pornography at all. It not only became the first bookstore of its kind, it embraced the new gay and lesbian culture, and brought a new sense of pride to the neighborhood.

Perhaps even more importantly, it recognized the community as a viable consumer base, with new interests and different viewpoints. Rodwell's store may very well have served as the initial impetus for major industries to start taking note of the marketing and advertising possibilities this brave new world might afford them. People were now walking out of the closet and into a gay bookstore to buy serious books about others like themselves, and oh boy, did they have disposable income. And though the Oscar Wilde Bookstore would suffer through graffiti and swastikas sprayed on the store throughout the coming decades, in years to come, corporations eventually tackled the marketing possibilities and reaped the profits of selling to this important audience.

In Washington, D.C., Lambda Rising bookstore would soon follow, opening in 1974 with 250 titles available. By 1975, local TV viewers were stunned to see a commercial for this new gay bookstore entering their predominantly straight homes. And years later, when Oscar Wilde was on the verge of closing after Craig Rodwell's death, it was Lambda Rising owner Deacon Maccubbin who bought the Greenwich Village landmark, assuring its survival. Survive—and flourish—it did, staying open continuously without missing even one day, serving an ever more growing community, and acting as a beacon around the world for others to follow in Craig Rodwell's very brave footsteps.

THE NAMES PROJECT AIDS MEMORIAL QUILT

IT WEIGHS FIFTY TONS NOW. It's considered the largest community arts project in the world. Sadly, it is now so unwieldy that it hasn't been displayed in its entirety in more than ten years. It's long been called just "The Quilt," and it may be the most joyful representation of death in history.

Cleve Jones, a friend and once an intern of San Francisco City Supervisor Harvey Milk, is responsible for this paean to fallen friends. The idea came to him after he and a friend handed out cardboard placards to marchers at a 1985 candlelight memorial service for Milk, asking them to write down the name of someone they knew who had died of AIDS. People wrote not just names, but messages, prayers, heartfelt thoughts. They taped several together and hung them from a window in the federal building in San Francisco, and it suddenly brought back one of Jones' earliest memories—his grandmother's quilt. By 1987, Jones had made the first panel for his friend Marvin Feldman, and this incredible portable monument began to come to life.

Each panel of the quilt, which numbers over 46,000 pieces, is extremely personal, with some unique elements sewn on and into the panels. Bubble wrap, pearls, flip-flops, hair, cremation ashes, jock-straps, crystals, mink and thousands of other items have made it a veritable traveling museum.

The last time the quilt was shown in toto was in Washington, D.C., in 1996. More than 1,000 panels have been added to the memorial since then: during the height of the AIDS epidemic, more than fifty panels a week were coming in. The quilt is maintained by The NAMES Project Foundation headquartered in Atlanta, Georgia, with over twenty chapters in the United States and forty affiliate organizations around the world. Its power has become universal in a way Cleve Jones could never have guessed. A documentary, *Common Threads: Stories from the Quilt,* won an Academy Award in 1989, the same year the quilt itself was nominated for the Nobel Peace Prize. A musical piece has been composed in its honor. In 2006, a youth project in Vancouver began a Digital Quilt: In fact, the idea of a "Names Project" has morphed into a way various groups have chosen as a tool for remembrance. There is a Holocaust names project and a Native tribe names projects (and many of far lesser fame). Portions of the quilt—a long way from Cleve Jones' grandmother's inspirational hand-iwork—constantly travel around the world: from high schools to temples, hospitals to shopping malls, offices to museums, it makes nearly 2,000 appearances a year. All from one man trying to find a special way to commemorate a friend.

The Portable Queer

OUR WORLD

POLARI

"How bona to vada your eek!"

NEXT TIME SOMEONE SAYS that to you (which could very well also be the first time anyone has *ever* said it to you), be cool. It's no threat—it's not even an insult. It's Polari, and in fact the above phrase is a compliment that means *"How nice to see your face!"*

Polari–sometimes seen as Parlyaree, from the Italian "parlare," to talk–dates back to the seventeenth century, when it gained use among carnival and fair-ground workers throughout Europe. This popularity among such transient workers explains the variety of linguistic touches that it includes: there's a little Yiddish, some Lingua Franca, backslang, Italian, sailor slang, Thieves' cant, and 1960s drug slang, to mention just a few. Originally a code language of only about twenty words, linguistic experts say it has now grown to 400-500 words.

It finally landed in London in the late nineteenth century, where it became all the rage in the theater world. From there, it was a nanosecond before it was part of the gay subculture, serving a strangely two-pronged purpose. Polari became a secret language for gay men, and thus a way to share and confide to other gay people in public, without being understood by heterosexuals. In this way it kept gays separate from straights. Yet at the same time it made homosexuality like a secret club, bringing people together. So it also protected homosexuals—while outing them at the same time. But it did the trick very nicely from the Oscar Wilde years to the decriminalization of homosexuality with the Sexual Offences Act in 1967.

By then a popular British radio show called "Round the Horne" had introduced the world to two campy characters named Julian and Sandy, and they singlehandedly kept Polari from becoming extinct. Even the 1998 film *Velvet Goldmine* featured a scene entirely spoken in Polari, thanks to the duo's popularity. After a fall from grace for the dialect towards the end of the twentieth century, it seems to be back in fashion among some of the younger queers. Enough to list some of its most important words here:

AJAX	*nearby*
AUNT NELLS	*ears*
BALONIE	*garbage*
BEVVY	*drink, cocktail*
BIJOU	*small*
BLAG	*pick up*
BONA	*good*
CHARPERING OMI	*policeman*
CHARVER	*to have sex*
CHAVIES	*boys, children*
COD	*vile, fake*
COLIN	*erection*
COTTAGING	*bathroom sex*
DOG AND BONE	*telephone*
DOLLY	*nice*
DRAG	*clothes*
EEF (ECAF)	*face*
FANTABULOSA	*fabulous*
FEELE	*child*
GELT	*money*
JUBES	*breasts*
LATTIE	*house*
LILLY	*police*

MANGARIE	*food*
MEESE	*ugly*
NAFF	*dull, hetero (acronym: not available for fucking)*
NANTY	*none*
NANTY DINARLY	*penniless*
NISHTA	*nothing*
OGLES	*eyes*
OMI	*man*
OMIPALONE	*homosexual*
PALONE	*woman*
PALONE-OMI	*lesbian*
RIAH	*hair*
SLAP	*makeup*
SO	*homosexual ("Is he so?")*
TRADE	*sex partner*
TROLL	*walk*
VADA	*see*
VOGUE	*cigarette*
ZHOOSH	*style hair, tart up*

1 *una*

2 *dewey*

3 *tray*

4 *quattro (quarter)*

5 *chunker*

6 *sayi*

7 *setter*

8 *otter*

9 *nobba*

10 *daiture*

COMING OUT

IF YOU THINK IT used to mean just debutantes until National Coming Out Day came along, think again. Coming out is by no means a new concept. People have always come out of the closet, of course, but it was way back in 1869 that the man considered the world's first homosexual rights advocate, Karl Heinrich Ulrichs, began to encourage it as a means of feeling free. Even then—or perhaps *because* of the way the world was then—Ulrichs realized that invisibility was the major obstacle in forming a community.

And he was soon followed by other believers; in 1906, Irwin Bloch, a German-Jewish doctor, began to suggest to elderly homosexuals that they open themselves up to their families and acquaintances. By 1914, Dr. Magnus Hirschfeld, a sexologist and homosexual activist, promoted the idea in his book, *The Homosexuality of Men and Women.* Even the conservative Mattachine Society, upon a change in leadership in 1953, loosened up and began to urge its members to come out and move not only into the public eye but into the political arena as well.

Then along came an ordinary guy, who, like so many ordinary guys do, did something extraordinary. His name was Frank Kemeny, and he'd been outed in the Army and subsequently fired. He did not go quietly: he fought his dismissal from the armed services all the way to the U.S. Supreme Court. And along the way he made up a slogan, which people actually began to take to the streets: "Gay is Good."

By 1979, a decade had passed since the Stonewall Riots, and gay political organizations were beginning to take serious hold both around the country and around the world. Still, the social mores of the world seemed not that much changed to LGBT people; they were beginning to come out of the closet in droves, yet understanding little of the process emotionally. It was at this point that Australian sexologist and clinical psychologist Dr. Vivienne Cass presented the Cass Model, the most commonly used system of outlining the six stages of gay and lesbian identity development:

IDENTITY CONFUSION: *"Could I be gay?" A time of self-exploration*

IDENTITY COMPARISON: *accepting the possibility and dealing with possible social alienation*

IDENTITY TOLERANCE: *"I am not the only one;" person seeks out others*

IDENTITY ACCEPTANCE: *has positive feelings about being gay rather than just self-toleration*

IDENTITY PRIDE: *often the time when the actual Coming Out happens; person divides the world into heterosexual and homosexual*

IDENTITY SYNTHESIS: *being gay synthesizes itself into the person's entire personality, so that being gay is only one part of the self*

"Coming Out" had become almost an official rite of passage. So in 1988, at the Second National March on Washington for Lesbian and Gay Rights, Jean O'Leary and Dr. Robert Eichberg founded National Coming Out Day. Held in the United States every October 11 (and international in its scope and participation on other specific days around the world), this project promotes awareness of the depth and reach of the LGBT community, and demonstrates the inclusion one feels being part of that community. Conventional wisdom is that coming out to a heterosexual friend or relative often aids the straight person's view and understanding of homosexuality, adding one more friend to our list. LGBTs and their coming-out friends often identify themselves by wearing a pink triangle, a lambda sign, or clothing and jewelry featuring the freedom rainbow.

GAY BATHHOUSES

IT'S A PRETTY GOOD BET that as long as there have been public baths, with people of the same sex milling about in the nude, there has been gay sex on the premises. It's certainly likely that it was prevalent during the more homosexually permissive cultures in ancient Greece and Rome, but by the Middle Ages, social mores had become more stringent. Records exist about a raid on a bathhouse as early as fifteenth century Florence; from 1492–1494, forty-four men were arrested for homosexual relations in such venues. In 1876 France, police took down a Parisian bathhouse on the Rue de Faubourg-Poissonniere and left with six men, aged fourteen to twenty-two. The first American arrests did not occur until 1903 at the Ariston Hotel Baths: twenty-six men were brought in, and twelve of them were brought to trial on sodomy charges. Seven of these men went to prison—receiving sentences of four to twenty years.

Still, in spite of the raids, things percolated along quite nicely in the bathhouse biz. In 1880s New York, the Everard—and yes, everyone *did* call it the "Everhard"—opened and was evidently such a good investment that the Gershwin brothers, Ira and George, bought it in 1916. And the famed Jermyn Street Turkish Bath in London was open for well over a century, from 1857 into the 1970s (Rock Hudson was a frequent visitor). Coney Island even had two hot bathhouses in the 1930s, Stauch's and Claridges—talk about a full-service amusement park!

The need for privacy exacerbated the popularity of the gay bathhouse as the twentieth century took hold. Cities were growing at an exponential rate, and places to meet in secret were getting harder and harder to find. Public bathrooms, alleys, parks, movie theaters, and expensive hotel rooms became less of an option as police began to regularly take action against huddled couples in the dark corners of these new metropolises. Soon even the YMCA cracked down, and though some straight owners of predominantly straight bathhouses called in the cops or private security guards to keep the clientele heterosexual, others began to see the huge profits afforded by a gay clientele. Discreet gay sex at bathhouses became not-so-discreet, and the homosexual customers were suddenly the norm.

The truth was that as the twentieth century progressed, cruising spots were dangerous...and a bathhouse was the one place it was safe to be gay.

By the 1950s, at least in the U.S., bathhouses were

starting to pop up for use by a gay clientele exclusively. In many cities, as long as there was no ruckus, police were happy to turn a blind eye to them and even happier to arrest fewer people having sex in spots on their beats. In San Francisco, the fledgling Mattachine Society was printing a guide to the bars and baths as early as 1954. And by 1965, a man named Jack Campbell—from Cleveland, of all places—decided gay ownership and less sleazy surroundings would make a difference to both his clientele and his bottom line. He and his partners started the Club Bath Chain, with TVs, Jacuzzis, carpeting, vending machines and the works: by 1973 they had 500,000 card-carrying members.

The 1970s were a circus. In Los Angeles, lines formed around the block to get into the 8709 Bathhouse, a place where it was so easy to buy drugs it was called "The Pharmacy." Owners were tricking out the baths with pools, discos, doctors on call for STD consults, orgy rooms—one even had a monster truck for clients to have sex in the cab, and a fake cell to fantasize prison sex.

Historically, perhaps the most famous bathhouse

was the Continental Baths in New York. You'd have to have been under a rock since 1970 to not know that Bette Midler debuted there: but most don't know that author Rita Mae Brown snuck in disguised as a man one night in 1975, and feminist politician Bella Abzug campaigned there, giving a gay rights speech that brought down the house. By now many of the baths—or "the tubs," as they were also called—were such a part of a city's gay culture that political organizations were even doing voter registration on the premises.

The fantasy was about to end, of course, in the most devastating way possible. The advent of AIDS, coupled with early fears of how easily the HIV virus might be spread, sent shock waves around the world. Extremely divisive fights began—the very thing the community did not need—and lengthy discussions about shutting down the bathhouses as hothouses of viral spread ensued. By 1984 the baths were closed down in San Francisco altogether; New York City followed a year later.

Much has changed since then, of course. The following was uttered by gay activist Dennis Altman in the 1970s, and though clearly inflation has taken hold, perhaps the fear of sexual harassment at the office has alleviated some:

"A gay man with $15 can get both sex and entertainment of the Continental and know he is mixing with the beautiful people. He might still turn up to work on Monday and be fired for being a fag."

SITUATIONAL HOMOSEXUALITY

LIFE HAS A WAY OF serving up changes—some good, some not so much. Along the way, occasions present themselves to people that cause them to modify their lifestyles—even their very lives. Such is the case with what is called situational homosexuality, sexual behavior that is not the norm for a particular person, not true to their basic sexual desires.

Situational homosexuality occurs most often when people find themselves in a single-sex environment for a lengthy period of time. The participant is not necessarily compelled to have relations with someone of their own sex; sometimes it is simply that it is permitted or encouraged. Or that it's just there.

Prisons are one of the most common venues for situational homosexuality—sometimes also called behavioral bisexuality. In a prison situation, the participant is often coerced into a homosexual relationship, though in his or her prior life they had been completely heterosexual. Jailhouse sex differs from other situational homosexuality because it often includes rape. For long periods of time, prisoners can be so intimidated that they pretend they are acquiescent; in truth, they have literally become sex slaves. Danger, and the certainty that they will be harmed, is the overriding fear for them. Homosexual sex in prison very often is based on control and dominance; generally, one partner is submissive. These are not always prisoner/prisoner relationships, either: prison guards are often the opposite sex of their charges, and are involved with—and the dominant partner in—heterosexual relationships.

Other types of situational homosexuality are not as fraught with power and control. The military sees much of this phenomenon, not only on its bases and posts, but especially with men aboard ships at sea for long intervals. Even more secretive are sexual relations among the residents of convents and monasteries.

Some of these relationships seem to be more about experimentation and marking time. Athletes on the road, boarding schools (both male and female) and college dorms seem to spawn people who are "temporarily gay." In fact, these time-sensitive couplings have become so common and gained such exposure that they have their own nicknames: prisons have "jailhouse turnouts," "bitches," "punks," and LURDs (Lesbians Until Release Date);" rugby teams have their "rugger-buggers;" and college students are tagged "BUG" (Bisexual Until Graduation") or "LUG" (Lesbian Until Graduation).

Some female athletes competing in team sports report that they not only have lesbian sex, but involve themselves in fewer heterosexual encounters while traveling with the other players; they insist "homosociability" builds team spirit and is a psychological boost. There's even a more politically correct term floating around for all of this: "heteroflexible."

There are also reports that Islamic men regularly

engage in same-sex encounters, though their religion not only forbids it, but deems sodomy punishable by death. But males and females are kept apart in a good part of daily life, and the Islamic men who participate in situational homosexuality are very much akin to the African-American experience of life on the Down Low; they do not consider themselves to be homosexual men in any way.

In a steamier turn of events, the emergence of sex tourism has also boosted the incidence of situational homosexuality. Now folks who lead their entire lives as heterosexuals at home can vacation in different exotic locales to live out their sexual fantasies with someone of their own gender. Many of these travelers—and this goes for straight travelers, too—are people who would never dream of hiring a prostitute in their own country, but don't feel themselves under the same moral confines in a country where such activity is legal or virtually ignored by local laws. Some of these destinations include Thailand, Brazil, the Dominican Republic, Costa Rica, Turkey, and Greece.

But the real question remains this: would we be

calling the majority of these occurrences "situational homosexuality" if bisexuality were more acceptable in our present society?

GAY PRIDE CELEBRATIONS

UNTIL THE STONEWALL RIOTS, "Pride" was not a word the gay community often used in connection with themselves. Inequality; invisibility, maybe; discrimination, certainly. But the actions and reactions of the LGBT people who finally said "No more" that night in 1969 on New York City's Christopher Street changed everything. Not only did much of the modern gay movement arise out of the events of what happened there, but exactly a year later, it birthed something new and shiny: Pride.

Borne out of Pride, one of the seven deadly sins, came Pride, the gay celebration. On June 28, 1970, the Gay Liberation Front led a march organized by bisexual activist Brenda Howard—the "Mother of Pride"—from New York's Greenwich Village to Central Park. It was initially called the Christopher Street Liberation Day March; eventually called the

Gay Pride Parade, it would later reverse its route so that the march would end outside the Stonewall Inn, which is still in business to this day. And wouldn't you know it: the Pride parade is the only one in Manhattan all year long that goes *down* Fifth Avenue. Los Angeles and San Francisco both held marches in 1970 as well, and in a return to the Summer of Love feeling, San Francisco even added a "gay-in." Soon the idea caught on in other cities throughout the United States, and before long June became a month-long Gay Pride celebration from coast to coast.

Traditionally a Pride parade runs the gamut of the community's diversity. From LGBT political organizations to floats chock-a-block with go-go boys, from popular bars to AIDS activists, there's a lot to love and usually plenty for conservatives to hate. Local Dykes on Bikes motorcycle groups often lead off the parades, offering annual fodder for six o'clock-news watchers everywhere.

All over the world, gay celebrations have begun to take hold in the month of June—some more successfully than others. In Moscow in spring 2007, gay and lesbian Russians attempted to organize a Gay

Pride march with a small, but brave, crowd of fewer than fifty people. Dissenters and police were there to meet them, and the organizers of the "satanic march" were arrested. People carried signs in the street: "For Russia Without Russophobes;" "Russia Without Sodomites;" "Buggery Not for Russians." A similar reaction greeted LGBT paraders in Belgrade in 2001. A peaceful march turned into mayhem, with skinheads, soccer fans, even men of the cloth joined to abort the planned festivities. As of this writing, there has not been a successful march in Belgrade.

There are more hopeful stories, like the first Pride march in Taipei in 2003. Though homosexuality remains a taboo in Taiwan, the good news is that the mayor attended the event; the sad news is that many marchers wore masks, because they were so fearful of being recognized. Some Eastern European countries still outlaw any sort of LGBT gatherings, and other places are too treacherous to chance a topic so hot.

Still, celebration of LGBT freedom has spread worldwide and is gaining momentum, promoting tolerance and understanding, campaigning for equal rights, and simply having a damn good time. From

Cape Town to Tokyo, Bangkok to Brussels, Helsinki, Berlin (all over Germany—in fact in many cities there it's called Christopher Street Day), Dublin, Reykjavik, Warsaw, Oslo, Edinburgh, Lima, Beirut, Montreal, Sydney, Istanbul, and many more, the freedom flag flies in June.

GAY GAMES

THEY'RE NOT SUPPOSED TO be about gold medals, nationalism, or for that matter, even being gay. The goals of the Gay Games have always been to promote inclusion (so inclusive you don't have to actually be gay to play), participate in sporting events with others, and define your personal best.

Founded by Tom Waddell, a medical doctor and 1968 Olympic decathlon athlete, the contests were originally known as the Gay Olympics. But apparently not everyone was all for inclusion: just a few weeks before the first Gay Games in San Francisco in 1982, the United States Olympic Committee slapped a suit on the games to force the new competition to change its name. The USOC insisted the word "Olympics" be dropped, and flat-out homophobia seemed to be at the bottom of it. There were the Special Olympics, of course, but there were also many other contests using the sacred "O Word"—like Police Olympics, Dog Olympics, Nude Olympics, even the Nebraska Rat Olympics—and the USOC had never lifted a finger before to put a halt to its usage. It seemed like a personal vendetta: all promotional materials, merchandise, advertising, signage and the like had to be scrapped, and the entire event renamed in order for the show to go on in less than three weeks' time. And go on it did.

They came. They came from all over the world, from countries where just *being* gay is against the law, sometimes punishable by death. There were 1,600 athletes at the first Games competing in fourteen events; by 2006 in Chicago, there were 12,500 athletes, nearly 150,000 spectators, and thirty-one events in which to compete.

However, much more has changed over the years for the Gay Games besides the size of the crowds and the number of events. In 1987, Tom Waddell died of AIDS, a year after the second Gay Games took place, again in San Francisco. In 1989, a new governing body, the Federation of Gay Games (FGG), was formed to replace Waddell's original group, called San Francisco Arts and Athletics. The Games—which from the start have also included cultural events as well—wanted to explore a more international presence, and began to accept bids from cities all over the world. Vancouver hosted the 1990 Games, New York City had the Games in 1994, pumping up the already gargantuan plans to celebrate the 25th anniversary of the Stonewall Riots, and finally Amsterdam took on the Gay Games in 1998, the first city to do so outside of North America. Sydney followed in 2002, with Montreal named as host city for the 2006 Games.

The Games have never been a financial success as of this writing, even with the aid of the host cities and several high-profile sponsors. After September 11, and with the world in a more conservative financial place, the FGG voiced their concerns to the Montreal organizing committee that they believed the budget and size of the event needed to be held more in check. An agreement could not be reached, and the FGG decided to move the 2006 Games to second choice

Chicago. This spawned both a nasty schism in gay athletics and a new organization: World Outgames, sponsored by the Gay and Lesbian International Sport Association, which continued to plan for a fete in Montreal in 2006. Scheduled only a week apart, this caused many athletes to have to choose between the two sportsfests, causing a serious community rift and huge financial problems for both.

Both the Gay Games and World Outgames plan to continue to sponsor international sports competitions, opting for different years for each set of games, but it remains to be seen how this athletic catfight will play out.

OUTING

"OUT OF THE CLOSETS, into the streets!"

A war cry that sounds almost dated now, it harkens back only to the United States in the 1970s. Angry "gay-libbers" after the Stonewall Riots were desperate for others to join the cause and help the burgeoning movement. Guilt seemed like a good motivator, and "coming out" of the closet would help.

Gossiping about someone's sexual preferences is as old as time, but most likely the first near-usage of the term "outing" came from historian Taylor Branch, who predicted in 1982 that homosexual politicians may well find themselves compromised by the gay public if they did not come to their aid politically. "Outage," as Branch called it, could harm their careers.

But the twentieth century proved Germany to be more open in its view of homosexuality. Pre-World War II Berlin was a hotbed of gay life, so it's no surprise that it was liberal German journalists who "outed" some of Kaiser Wilhelm II's cabinet members way back in 1907. Even more famous was the outing—and assassination—in 1934 of Hitler's right-hand man and founder of the SA, Ernst Röhm.

The first public outing by a gay activist was of Senator Mark Hatfield in 1989 by a group led by Michael Petrelis. Hatfield was supporting legislation by right-wing extremist Senator Jesse Helms. Suddenly it was clear that Taylor Branch had been right on the mark. In that same year *OutWeek* magazine began publication, and *über*outer Michelangelo Signorile began the practice of outing in earnest, including the recently deceased financial mogul Malcolm Forbes.

In their book *Outing: Shattering the Conspiracy of Silence*, Walter Johansson and William A. Percy note that there are different parameters that most activists agree should be adhered to for outing, though in actual practice they vary quite widely:

1: *Hypocrites only, and only when they actively oppose gay rights and interests;*

2: *Outing passive accomplices who help run homophobic institutions;*

3: *Prominent individuals whose outing would shatter stereotypes and compel the public to reconsider its attitude on homosexuality;*

4: *Only the dead.*

A generation after it was given a name, outing has eased its way into our language to enjoy a much wider usage. It is used generally to mean giving away a secret about a person's life or personality which they wish to keep hidden. Seems even our lexicon is coming out of the closets and into the streets.

REPARATIVE THEORY

CONVENTIONAL WISDOM holds that one's sexual orientation is a part of one's whole—unchangeable—and not a matter of just changing one's mind. In fact, coercion can be extremely harmful to a person's psyche. But that doesn't stop people from trying to modify others around them: families, clergy, and conservative groups have come to think it is not only their business but their right and their mission to actually attempt to change someone's sexuality.

It's called reparative therapy, or sometimes conversion therapy, or—of all things—reorientation therapy, and it's all dedicated to trying to change people's sexuality and to live a life as a heterosexual. Through several different techniques, those who practice these therapies attempt to eliminate not only homosexual behavior, but homosexual desires as well.

By the later nineteenth century, sexologists had begun to ply their wares. Richard von Krafft-Ebing cited homosexuality as a deviant sexual practice, though he did not blame the individual for his sexual orientation; Krafft-Ebing believed that homosexuality was congenital, or what he called "acquired inversion." Sexologist Havelock Ellis, in his book *Sexual Inversion*, was convinced that it was a combination of biological factors and a person's upbringing that determined sexuality. But in this fairly new business of psychology, the majority of practitioners determined that it was a physical and psychological malady, often calling it the "third sex." And as for ways to cure it, they were willing to try anything on a patient: aversion therapy, electric shock therapy, psychoanalysis, brain surgery, castration, nausea-producing drugs, administration of the drug Metrazol to induce convulsion, even breast amputation. Some of the more religiously based attempts add prayer and religious counseling to the mix.

When these cannibalistic regimens didn't work, sexologists and their cohorts—still convinced that homosexuality was a psychological aberration and curable condition—resorted to attempting to persuade the public that they could change people who were unhappy with their current "sick" sexual orientation. They insisted that it was a choice.

This train of psychological thought has gained

popularity now and again throughout the last century, but has never been more under fire since the advent of camps devoted to making "ex-gays" of teenagers. Reparative therapist groups, at the behest of parents whose children are still under age, force youngsters into programs that have been found on occasion to be so destructive to a teen's psyche that the camps are being charged with child abuse, in accordance to the statutes in several states.

The gay rights movement points to the religious right as the source for much of this problem. The National Gay and Lesbian Task Force has said it is "the Christian Right repackag[ing] its anti-gay campaign in kinder, gentler terms. Instead of simply denouncing homosexuals as morally and socially corrupt, the Christian Right has now shifted to a strategy of emphasizing... the ex-gay movement. Behind this mask of compassion, however, the goal, remains the same: to roll back legal protections for lesbian, gay, bisexual, and transgender people."

Of course, the American Psychiatric Association declassified homosexuality as a disease in 1973. In 1997, the American Psychological Association went even further in laying out their principles concerning conversion, or reparative, therapies:

> *Homosexuality is not a mental disorder and the APA opposes all portrayals of lesbian, gay and bisexual people as mentally ill and in need of treatment due to their sexual orientation;*
> *Psychologists do not knowingly participate in or condone discriminatory practices with lesbian, gay and bisexual clients;*
> *Psychologists respect the rights of individuals, including lesbian, gay and bisexual clients to privacy, confidentiality, self-determination and autonomy;*
> *Psychologists obtain appropriate informed consent to therapy in their work with lesbian, gay and bisexual clients.*

Happily, as in most movements, there are dissatisfied customers. Where there are ex-gays, there are also ex-ex-gays. Though the latter are not all necessarily at peace with the fact that they are, and will remain, gay (and many do wish they were heterosexuals), they have all been convinced that there is no way to forcibly change one's sexuality, and are adamant about carrying this message to the public. As Popeye would preach: "I yam what I yam."

GAYS IN THE MILITARY

THE UNITED STATES may be the most vocal country about their attitude on gays in the military—with "Don't Ask, Don't Tell" they certainly have the best sound bite—but many other countries around the world employ rules equally as harsh. Some are even more stringent. Of the twenty-five countries that are military participants in NATO, nearly all allow gays and lesbians to serve; in Britain and France they can soldier on without repercussion. Russia's policy is very much akin to the United States' "see no evil" attitude, while the following countries outlaw gays in the military altogether:

BRAZIL	PHILIPPINES
CHINA	SAUDI ARABIA
CUBA	SYRIA

EGYPT   VENEZUELA
IRAN   YEMEN
          NORTH KOREA

As for the U.S. policy, the strict insistence to fighting without the help of homosexuals actually dates back to the Revolutionary War. In 1778, General George Washington approved the dismissal of Lieutenant Gotthold Frederick Enslin, convicted of sodomy and perjury. In World War II, soldiers found to be gay were dishonorably discharged, and sent back to a civilian life where they were denied veterans' benefits. They also often had trouble finding employment: if their military dismissal papers read "Section 8," employers turned them away, knowing the discharge was most likely the result of a homosexual incident.

Often in the past, especially during the time of the Vietnam War, gay personnel relied on a humiliating "queen for a day" rule, which allowed someone accused of committing a homosexual act the opportunity to prove that it was a single aberrant situation.

In 1993, President Bill Clinton, who had promised during his presidential campaign to do away with a ban on gays in the U.S. military, caved to the conservatives. His compromise, commonly known as "Don't Ask, Don't Tell," devised by former General and then-Secretary of State Colin Powell, left the LGBT community up in arms. Formally called Pub.L. 103-160 (10 U.S.C. § 654), this policy calls for investigations and possible dismissal from the armed forces if a soldier:

> *makes a statement that they are lesbian, gay or bisexual*
> *engages in physical contact with someone of the same sex for the purposes of sexual gratification*
> *marries, or attempts to marry, someone of the same sex*

Paradoxically, if one hides their sexual orientation while in the service, a superior officer is not allowed to open an investigation about their sexuality.

In 1957, there was a brief moment when it

seemed like military attitudes might loosen up. Commissioned by the U.S. Navy, the Crittenden Report found that gays were no more likely to be a security risk than anyone else, and that there was no "visible supporting data to support the conclusion that gays and lesbians cannot acceptably serve in the military." Unfortunately, due to the social mores in the country and its general acceptance of homosexuality at the time, the study stopped just short of recommending that gays and lesbians should be allowed to serve their country. Even today, the United States government's official stance is that gays in the military would lower morale, harm recruitment success, and undermine unit cohesion—although a 2005 *Boston Globe* poll showed that 79 percent of the American public saw no reason to exclude them.

Reports still say that harassment of alleged homosexuals in the military seems to continue unabated, including wrongful deaths like those of soldiers Allen Schindler and Barry Winchell, both killed due to this senseless law. Yet the U.S government seemed to be turning a blind eye to gay and lesbian soldiers as the conflict in the Middle East continued. Nearly 10,000 troops were discharged during the first ten years since "Don't Ask, Don't Tell" was put in place. Public consensus is that the military needs soldiers, and the number of those dismissed continues to lessen, from 1,227 in 2001 to 612 in 2006. Research based on the U.S. census guesstimates that there are 65,000 gays and lesbians in the military as of this writing: it seems suspicious that the number of dismissals has suddenly been cut in half. More like the government has found that it's cheaper and more useful to keep highly trained personnel, homosexual or not. If they could only admit it, they could almost call it equality.

LIFE ON THE DOWN LOW

"KEEP IT ON THE down low."

Used to be that phrase meant *Keep things quiet, Don't tell, This is just between you and me.* But in the last few years, its most popularized usage has been to identify a gay fringe group—though in the main, these men don't even consider themselves gay.

Life on the down low, or "The DL," as it's often called, is as old as sex itself. It implies that someone is going out on his or her lover or spouse. It's first known use referring to homosexual life is from a 1930 song, "Boy in the Boat," though in this case, oddly enough, it's all about lesbians. But a groundswell of talk about the down low really started up in 2001—and it nearly always pertained to African-American men.

The *Los Angeles Times* ran the first story about life on the down low in February 2001; by the end of the year, similar stories had appeared in many major news outlets, from the *New York Times* to *Essence* to *Vibe*. The focus of these stories was not just the gay subculture that had come to light, but a devastating accusation: that men on the down low were connected to the growing HIV/AIDS epidemic in the straight African-American community.

By 2003, these accusations were gaining a listenership, and two prominent black gay cultural critics finally spoke out: Jason King in the *Village Voice* and Frank Leon Roberts in the *San Francisco Chronicle*. They began to question the validity of these allegations. Now the interesting gay sidebar had become

a racial slur, and so far there was no statistical proof
that the spread of the virus had anything to do with
these men on the down low.

Then came Oprah, and the preceding coverage of
the issue seemed like a tempest in a tiny little teapot.
In April of 2004, a man named J.L. King appeared
on her show to discuss his soon-to-be-published tell-
all, *On the Down Low*. It caused an instant furor: it
seemed like black America had known about it all
along and just didn't want to talk about it, and white
America was hearing about these men—who identify themselves as straight black men who have sex
with other black men in secret on the side—for the
very first time. It also brought out into the open the
question of shame (a feeling that many LGBTs have
long been familiar with) that African-American men
suffer at the hands of a community where mascu-
linity and family play a huge part in a man's stature.
And worse, theories abounded that life on the down
low was a hotbed of unsafe sex. That black men were
destroying their own through their vanity.

Suddenly the down low was the hot new plot-
line of TV shows like *Law & Order* and *ER* and the

newest cocktail party joke. Even the Oscar-winning movie *Brokeback Mountain* was seen as a study on life on the DL.

It harmed the gay community, it caused a rift in the black community, and as of this writing, the Center for Disease Control has found no link between this formerly hidden subculture and the growth of HIV cases among straight black women.

The Portable Queer

SIGNS & SYMBOLS

GAY SYMBOLS

EVERY CULTURE, EVERY NATION, every people have their signs and symbols, ways to distinguish themselves from the rest of the world. In the last hundred years especially, as the LGBT community began to come out of the closet as a whole and compose their own specific identity, a new legacy of signs and symbols began to sprout up. These same years have seen the first opportunity and efforts to seriously record LGBT history as well, but often the particulars of historical incidents that have happened during even the last few decades have dimmed. For example, the chronology of events of the Stonewall Riots is often argued, and the beginnings of some of the most significant gay rights organizations, like the Gay Liberation Front and the Gay Activists' Alliance, are hazy. So, too, are the histories of some of the symbols of our culture—but that doesn't make the theories of their conception any less fascinating. Hence, a look at some of the symbols that mark our world.

THE PINK TRIANGLE

It's commonly known that Adolf Hitler devised a system of symbols for use in Nazi concentration camps to identify separate sects of prisoners. The Jews, of course, wore a yellow star, two triangles overlapped to form a Star of David. Green was used for regular prisoners, and red denoted a political prisoner. The pink triangle–in German, *rosa winkel*– identified male homosexuals (and pederasts, further associating gays with the public's idea of perversion). A lesser-known symbol was the black triangle, stitched on the uniforms of lesbians and some prisoners who were thought to exhibit antisocial behavioral characteristics. (A woman not willing to act as a wife and mother and further strengthen the Aryan race was, of course, considered antisocial.) There have even been some uncorroborated reports that a burgundy triangle existed for transgendered prisoners. The most reviled badge of all was a yellow star superimposed with a pink triangle, denoting a gay Jew.

But why were homosexuals so scorned by Hitler? Paragraph 175 had been in effect since 1871, forbidding homosexual acts, so there were no new legal implications. Der Fuhrer had friends and officers in high command who were homosexual—and of course rumors abound even today about Hitler's own sexual preferences. He made his reasoning quite clear in a 1937 speech to high-ranking SS officers: "If you further take into account the facts that I have not yet mentioned, namely that with a static number of women, we have two million men too few on account of those who fell in [World War I], then you can well imagine how this imbalance of two million homosexuals and two million war dead, or in other words a lack of about four million men capable of having sex, has upset the sexual balance sheet of Germany, and will result in a catastrophe."

This is what made homosexuality the ultimate sin: gay men would not be empowering and reproducing the Aryan race.

As many as 50,000 gay men may have lost their lives to the Third Reich in camps.

But the pink triangle has become what is called a "reclaimed" word or symbol; the same has happened with the word queer. "Reclaimed" is the term for when a group takes back something that has been used in a pejorative sense and gives it a new, positive meaning. This happened in the case of the pink triangle in the 1970s, when it was resurrected for use to promote the gay civil rights movement: repression had transformed into celebration. Its final reincarnation came in its use as a symbol for the gay political group ACT UP, when the pink triangle was inverted, indicating a promise to fight back rather than to ever again be persecuted.

THE RAINBOW FLAG

Russell Baker thought the gay community needed a symbol. Something that promoted hope, looked joyful, had a sort of eternal feeling. So in 1978, he hand-dyed and sewed the original rainbow flag, finishing it in time for its debut in the San Francisco Gay Freedom Day Parade on June 25. (It was carried by Justin Fox, lead singer of Last Blue Film.) Though we now see the rainbow flag most often with the six stripes commonly associated with an actual rainbow, Baker originally designed it with eight, and each stripe had a special meaning:

HOT PINK	*sexuality*
RED	*life*
ORANGE	*healing*
YELLOW	*sunlight*
GREEN	*nature*
TURQUOISE	*magic*
BLUE	*serenity*
VIOLET	*spirit*

Eventually the turquoise and pink stripes were dropped (the latter because not enough pink material could be found for the immediately hot, must-have item). The flag took on both new importance and popularity just a few months after that gay pride Parade, when openly gay San Francisco politician Harvey Milk was killed. Suddenly the rainbow flag began to dot the memorial services for Milk, and before long was a truly universal gay symbol.

Yet long before the flag "belonged" to the gay community, many versions of it were flown around the world for centuries, and for a wide variety of reasons. In fact, it is believed that the idea of displaying the spectrum as a celebratory tradition began with

God's promise to Noah; the rainbow in the sky he saw after the flood foretold that God would never punish His people in such a way again. Similar flags have also been flown in various cultures as a symbol of hope, diversity, and inclusiveness. It has even gained a more universal name in the last few years: the freedom flag. And the law is making sure citizens are free to fly it, too—at least in West Hollywood, California. In 1989, a landlord there took issue with tenant John Stout's right to fly the flag outside his home—and lost. Long wave the rainbow flag!

OTHER ICONS

LAMBDA: in the wake of Stonewall came the formation of New York City's Gay Activists Alliance. Looking for a unifying symbol, the Greek letter Lambda was chosen. This was meant, naturally, to both signal something to those in the know, yet also act as a sort of secret code. People—gay men especially—began to wear the Lambda sign as jewelry, tattoos, and the like, and could identify kindred souls without a word. It's said that Tom Doerr of the Gay

Activists Alliance chose the symbol because it was used in chemistry and physics to mean "a complete exchange of energy," an apt message for the nascent organization to send. Some remember that the purpose of using a Greek letter was that it could easily be mistaken for a straight men's fraternity letter, and thus allow gays to share their secret unnoticed by the majority of the population. But then fame got in the way: in 1974, the International Gay Rights Congress declared the Lambda the symbol for gay and lesbian rights worldwide in recognition of GAA's excellent work in the chaotic post-Stonewall years. The GAA was hesitant, as many other gay advocacy groups didn't have the same goals and practices as they did, but the deal was done—and the rest is history. Today it has also become the logo for Lambda Legal Defense and Education Fund and the Lambda Literary Foundation as well.

LABRYS: this double-headed ax is also a product of ancient times. Today used as a symbol of pride and power by lesbians, it is meant to be identical to the scepter used by Demeter, the goddess of the earth.

Mythology suggests that worship of both Demeter and Hecate—the goddess of the underworld—involved lesbian sex. The labrys is also said to have been a tool used by Amazon women.

CALAMUS: Walt Whitman used this plant as the centerpiece to his "Calamus" sequence of forty-five poems to represent homoerotic love. In Egypt in days of old, this wetland perennial was known as a powerful aphrodisiac; its leaves are scented and have been used through the centuries not only medicinally, but as a psychotropic drug.

LADSLOVE: English poets from the nineteenth and twentieth centuries used ladslove, a plant of the artemisia family, to symbolize homosexuality.

VIOLETS: another plant used to celebrate same-sex love, though primarily for lesbians; the gift of violets was common between women from the 1920s through the 1940s. And back in the sixteenth century, men and women who planned to never marry wore violets (what "never marry" means we'll most likely never know). But the origin seems to be from Sappho, the original Lesbian heroine. She described, in a poem, wearing garlands of violets with her lover.

THE HARE, HYENA, AND WEASEL: since the first century, these animals have been associated with male homosexuality. The source is from an epistle of Barnabas.

PINKY RING: during the 1950s through the 1970s, this was a fashionable accessory for the gay man (with apologies to the Mafia).

BLUE STAR: lesbians in the mid-twentieth century would sport this five-pointed tattoo, especially on the bicep. It was easily covered up from prying eyes during the daytime, but could be uncovered and shown off socializing at night.

PHOENIX: this mythical bird, which rises, erect like the penis, to resurrect itself again and again, has long been a symbol of homosexuality.

RED NECKTIE OR SCARF: wearing one of these in the early days of the twentieth century was often a wink and a nod to other homosexuals.

GREEN: in nineteenth-century England, it was well-known that the "wearing of the green" signaled a homosexual man, but ancient Romans evidently had the same idea. In its more modern renaissance, a common heads-up would be for men to wear a green carnation: in fact, this became the calling card of famed Irish playwright and gadabout homosexual Oscar Wilde. On the opening night of one of his plays, *Lady Windermere's Fan*, Wilde played a prank on his public. One of the play's stars, several of Wilde's friends in the audience, and Wilde himself all wore green carnations. When asked what this floral brotherhood meant, Wilde replied, "Nothing whatever, but that is just what nobody will guess." Apparently green cravats were popular with Parisian men around the same time, though there was also a theory that green did not mean homosexuality per se, but decadence.

LAVENDER RHINOCEROS: this gigantic mammal—painted lavender with a little red heart—began to appear in Boston subways in 1973. Since the rhino is a peaceful animal until threatened, activists figured it fit the bill perfectly as a mascot in a new post-Stonewall world; it has since become a symbol for the entire gay community, coast-to-coast.

RED RIBBON: known to the world as the AIDS ribbon, and the granddaddy of all the colored ribbons worn today. Visual AIDS, a group of New York art professionals, began the Red Ribbon Project in 1991 to raise awareness of the epidemic, and to attempt to provoke the government into providing more funding and monies for research. Frank Moore of Visual AIDS noted that red was chosen for its "connection to blood and the idea of passion—not only for anger, but for love, like a valentine." Jeremy Irons was the first celebrity televised wearing the ribbon that same year, when he hosted the Tony Awards; as time went by, even the general public began to feel that the Red Ribbon was perhaps suspiciously overused, and seemed to be becoming a celebrity accessory, quite possibly with no positive action being taken by those wearing it. One infamous incident had First Lady Barbara Bush sporting the ribbon at an event until she appeared standing next to the President: by that time it had mysteriously vanished from her dress.

WHITE RIBBON: the color was chosen to represent the innocence of youth; the White Ribbon campaign, called Gay Teen Suicide Awareness, was started by teen suicide survivor Xavier Neptus, himself a gay adolescent.

LAVENDER RIBBON: this ribbon is worn to raise the awareness of the countless lesbian mothers and gay fathers who are denied custody and visitation rights with their children due to the close-mindedness of heterosexual parents.

EQUALITY SIGN: the yellow "equals" sign on a dark blue background was designed by the Human Rights Campaign as their logo in the 1990s to signify equal rights for all people.

GREEN RIBBON: though it is widely worn as a call to action against any kind of abuse—especially child abuse—the LGBT community also wears it as a reminder of the prevalence of hate crimes and gay-bashing.

LAVENDER COLOR: it is believed that this became popular as the "gay color" because it is a combination of pink and blue, representing both gay men and lesbians. In fact, in the 1930s, the word "lavender" was slang for lesbian.

DOUBLE MOON: many Europeans, Germans especially, took umbrage when the pink triangle became a universal homosexual symbol. While the rest of the world viewed its use as a sign of gay strength and a fierce desire to put the tragedy of Hitler's treatment of homosexuals behind them, some longed for a new symbol. So in 1998 a new logo was born: two rainbow crescents, back-to-back, one slightly above the other. It is now used as a gay logo in many countries throughout Europe.

GENDER SYMBOLS: the astrological sign of Mercury is often seen as a symbol for transgendered people. It is taken from Greek mythology: the goddess of love, Aphrodite, had a child, Hermaphroditus, with Hermes, who is the Greek version of the Roman god Mercury. Obviously the word hermaphrodite—a person who possesses the sexual organs of both the male and the female—comes from the name of this mythological love child. An alternate transgender symbol is a combination of the male and female gender symbols, so that the spear and cross are both featured.

The usual gender symbols used to connote male and female are also taken from astrological signs. The male is Mars, and is said to stand for a shield and a spear. The female, a circle with a cross below it, is Venus. Double interlocking symbols of each have been used since the 1970s to represent gay men or lesbians, connoting their togetherness as couples. When feminism became a fighting force in the United States in the 1970s, they, too, began to use the two interlocking Venuses, and showed three of the interlocking astrological signs to indicate lesbians. At this point, both men and women's gender symbols began to appear in rainbow stripes, in order to differentiate them and show a sense of gay pride.

THE HISTORY OF GAY SLANG

SLANG OFTEN COMES into popular use for one of two reasons. It is either the invention of an interested group attempting to construct a language to hide an unpopular social aspect, or the invention of people who wish to ridicule the aforementioned group. Thus, for example, economic, racial, and sexual subcultures have taken a verbal beating throughout history, and homosexuals are by no means the least among them.

As time goes on and the particular slang becomes part of the language of the culture, it often paves the way for the group to which it refers to assimilate. At that point, certain words are used with pride to show ownership and inclusion. These words are often called reclaimed words, and in the gay culture the most obvious examples are probably the current usage of queer, faggot, and dyke. Like many reclaimed words, they are most often acceptably used only by the subculture in question.

A look at the history of several of homosexual culture's most used—and misused—words:

GAY: it is now so ingrained in the English-speaking world as a substitute for "homosexual" that its former use, as a synonym for *merry*, *bright*, *showy*, *lively* and like words, is nearly out of use. Gay as homosexual came into use nearly a century ago, when its meaning as *uninhibited* and *carefree* took on a sexual connotation, e.g., practicing more unusual sexual tastes, an "anything goes" sort of attitude.

It comes as no surprise that a passage from Gertrude Stein's *Miss Furr & Miss Skeene* may have been the first time the current usage of the word appeared in print: "They were quite regularly gay there....They were very regularly gay....To be regularly gay was to do every day the gay thing that they did every day."

QUEER: the word has always meant *suspicious*, *odd*, or *strange*, so it's not a real surprise that it ended up becoming a term of derision before being reclaimed as part of the gay lexicon. One of its first slang appearances was in the 1890s by the Marquess of Queensbury to his son, Lord Alfred "Bosie" Douglas, regarding his sexual relationship with playwright Oscar Wilde. Soon it was being uttered by heterosexuals to mean effeminate and homosexual men. Though it is presently used fairly commonly in the LGBT community, it is not totally reclaimed; some still take offense at it and see it as a highly politicized word.

Faggot or fag—the notion that it means "a bundle of sticks"—which was the very confusing definition we all found in the dictionary as kids—has nothing to do with it moving into the vernacular to mean homosexual. It's more likely that it hearkens back to the sixteenth century, when it stood for "old or unpleasant woman." Other age-old put-downs also use the fact of being a woman as an insult: *nancy*, *queen*, *mary*, and *nelly* are all derogatory words for a homosexual man.

DYKE: the origins of this word are less clear. It is said that the word "dike" appeared in 1710 newspaper stories about two women pirates who dressed as men, and the French work dike, meaning men's clothing, was used to describe them. Other thoughts have it as a shortened, colloquial version of hermaphrodite. Certainly by the 1920s, Harlem Renaissance novels were referring to lesbians as *bulldykers*, the "bull" adding an aggressive, masculine connotation to the word. It was not a compliment at the time, and is not considered totally reclaimed by all lesbians today.

DRAG: the present use of this word has a somewhat obvious and comical source. In days of yore, male stage actors played all the parts in a play—men's and women's both. Men playing women and costumed in long dresses found soon enough while rushing around backstage that their long skirts were getting caught on things and, well, dragging. These acting parts were known as "drag roles," and it wasn't long before the phrase became a homosexual slur.